CW00495646

OPTIONS MARKET

You will discover many options strategies that will help you take your first steps in this market.

David J. Paul

responsibility of the recipient reader. Under no circumstances will any legal responsibility or blame be held against the publisher for any reparation, damages, or monetary loss due to the information herein, either directly or indirectly.

Respective authors own all copyrights not held by the publisher.

The information herein is offered for informational purposes solely, and is universal as so. The presentation of the information is without contract or any type of guarantee assurance.

The trademarks that are used are without any consent, and the publication of the trademark is without permission or backing by the trademark owner. All trademarks and brands within this book are for clarifying purposes only and are the owned by the owners themselves, not affiliated with this document.

Table of Contents

OPTIONS MARKET

Chapter 1 In the money, out of the money

When trading options you're often going to hear the terms in the money and out of the money. We've defined them but lets briefly take a closer look at what they mean.

In the Money

In the money simply means that exercising the option would result in a profit. For a call option, that means that the current stock price has risen above the strike price.

If Acme Communications is trading at $100 a share, and you have a call option with a strike price of $60, that means that you're in the money and you can buy the shares at $60 and sell them for $100 in the market. The option contract is said to have an intrinsic value that is equal to the difference between the stock price and the strike price, that is $100-$60 = $40 is the intrinsic value.

When you automatically exercise your options

If you have enough cash in your brokerage account when the call option contract expires to cover the purchase of the underlying shares at the strike price, if the call option expires in the money, then you're going to purchase the stocks automatically. Of course, you can sell them right away for a profit or hold them, your choice at that point.

Out of the Money

When the strike price is higher than the market price of the underlying asset, the call option is said to be out of the money. A call option that is out of the money has no intrinsic value, but it may have time value. Any option that reaches the expiry is worthless if it's out of the money at that point. However, if it still has time value and the underlying asset has been increasing in value such that the option is closer to being in the money, then it may be valuable enough to sell the option to another investor, and they may purchase it from you at a higher price than you paid for the premium. So, remember here that we are talking about trading the option itself, and not the underlying stock. So if you sell the option to someone else, you may recoup all or part of the premium, or even make a profit on it, however, the investor who buys it from you will be the one who can exercise the right to buy the stocks and/or hold the option until the expiration date.

Chapter 2 Buying and Selling Puts

So far, we've talked exclusively about buying and selling call options. Generally speaking, this is a better option for beginning traders. Our belief is that starting out selling covered call options, then moving on to limited purchases of call options is the best way to get started in options trading. Once you gain experience in that, you can move on to trading options themselves and also with buying and selling put options.

Let's quickly review what's involved in puts. A put is a bet on a decrease in stock price. Truthfully, puts aren't really all that different than calls, because a call is based on an educated hunch that some stock is going to go up in price in the coming weeks or months. A put is a bet that the opposite will occur, in other words, that the stock market price is going to decrease in the coming weeks or months.

First, let's look at how in-the-money and out-of-the-money are defined for puts.

How a Put Option Works

A put option from the buyer's perspective is the option to sell the underlying stock asset at a pre-agreed strike price. In this case, the bet you're making as the buyer of the contract is that the stock price is going to drop in value, and then you can sell the shares to the seller of the put contract at a higher price.

Suppose there is a pharmaceutical company called Theran Nose. Let's say that the shares are currently trading at $100, but there is bad news swirling around. You've studied the situation and are confident the stock will fall and do so more than dropping to $70. You find a seller of a put contract that doesn't think it's going to drop that much by the expiration date, and so they sell you the put option with a $70 strike price.

Then a week before the expiration date, the price crashes to $40 a share. In the case of a put, the seller of the put MUST purchase the shares from you. So, you buy the stock at $40 a share, and then you sell the shares to the seller at $70 a share. Needless to say, they will be seriously irritated, but you made a better bet and come out with a profit of $30 a share.

In the Money

In the case of a put option, when the stock price is below the strike price, it is said to be in the money. If the strike price is $150, and the stock price is $100, the put option has an intrinsic value of $50. The buyer of the put can buy the stock at $100 a share and sell it for $150 a share.

Out of the money

In the case of a put, if the market price is above the strike price, then there is no intrinsic value. In an analogous fashion to that we've seen for call options, however, if the contract has time value, then it may still be possible to profit from the contract. You may be able to sell it to another investor and get some or all of your premium back, or if there is enough time value, and it looks like even though the stock has yet to decline below the strike price that there are decent odds that it will, then you might get lucky and find an investor who will buy the option contract from you.

Using Puts as Insurance

So far, we've talked about put options in terms of speculating. That is, over the short-term interval of the contract, you believe that the underlying stock is going to drop in price and do so by dropping below the strike price. However, a put option can also be used as a form of insurance for securities in your portfolio. This can work for index funds or for individual stocks.

Suppose you have a stock that you're hoping to hold for the long term. Its prospects are uncertain, so there is a chance that you could lose a lot of money. Maybe you've invested in 1,000 shares. If you do nothing and the stock tanks, then you're out of luck. For the sake of example, we'll say that you bought the stock at $10 a share, for a total price of $10,000.

Then after some bad news, it tanks, dropping to $2 a share. Now you're left with an investment worth just $2,000, and you lost $8,000. Your only hope is to either sell now and cut your losses or hold it and hope that things get better in the future.

Another alternative is to buy some put contracts on the stock. Let's say the contracts have a premium of $0.56, so it costs $56 to buy a put contract for 100 shares. Altogether, you'll have to invest $560 to buy enough to cover your entire investment.

Now suppose that they came with a strike price of $7.

The stock tanks to $2 a share. You can then sell your shares at $7 to the seller of the puts. That gives you $7,000 back. Incorporating the cost of the premium, you've recovered $6,440.

Although you haven't recovered all of your losses, it's certainly true that having $6,440 is far better than only being able to recoup $2,000. We see how a put acting as an insurance policy can help protect our existing investments.

Speculating with Puts

Speculating with puts is trickier than doing so with call options. In fact, the most famous options traders are those who "short" a stock, and there is a good reason. Knowing which stocks are going to fall might seem obvious, but it doesn't always work that way. Without getting inside information, which of course is illegal, you're going to have to make educated guesses. In other words, the advice here is basically the same as it is with calls. You'll have to study the markets and watch all the financial news networks to find out what companies have prospects for heading into a downturn. Overall, of course, a bear market or recession will be the best time to look for a prospect for put options.

Chapter 3 Profit with Options Strategies and Positions

Because you can buy and sell options and options come in two flavors, calls that benefit from a rise in share prices and puts that benefit from a decline in share prices, one of the major advantages of options trading is that you can do a lot of different things that simply are not possible when it comes to trading stocks. This gives rise to many different strategies that can be utilized to minimize losses. Some of the strategies also minimize potential profits, but with practically guaranteed earnings, most people are willing to make that trade-off. Keep in mind that your broker may require a higher trading level to execute some of the strategies, and so not all traders may be able to enter into all of these trades without gaining more experience first. Note that spreads involve buying and selling options simultaneously so will require level 3 trading status.

Long Straddle

A straddle involves buying a call and a put option for the same stock, with the same expiration date and the same strike price. Long simply means we buy both options.

Let's look at a few scenarios. For our examples, we will assume a share price of $190, implied volatility of 24%, and imagine that the options are purchased with 30 days to expiration.

Suppose that we buy options with a strike price of $180. A call will be $11.60, and the put will be $1.56. The total investment is $13.16 (x 100 = $1,316).

In the first scenario, suppose that share price rises by $5 within 14 days. At this point, the put is $0.22, and the call has risen to $15.24. We can close our positions (sell both, the put at the loss) and earn $15.46 (x 100 = $1,546). Our profit is $230.

If instead, the share price had dropped, if it ends up at the money, then we'd be facing a loss. The call and put options would be priced at $3.62 and $3.60 respectively, leaving us with a total of $7.22. We would sell and take the loss or wait it out to see where the price moved in the coming days.

To make a profit from a drop in share price, it would have to drop to less than $167 a share. This example illustrates that buying a straddle that is strongly in the money for the call option strongly favors the call, in that the share price would have to drop considerably for the put to be profitable. The reverse would be true if we chose a strike price in such a way as to have an in the money put. So a move to a lower share price would make the put quite profitable, but a move to a higher price would have to be dramatic to make the call, and therefore the trade, profitable.

Following the earlier example, if the share price were $190 and we bought a call and a put at the money with 30 days to expiration, the cost would be $3.82 + $3.80 = $7.62, for a total investment of $762.

After 14 days, if the share price had risen to $195, the call would be $6.88, and the put $1.85, so we could sell both for $8.73, or a total of $873, giving a profit of $153. The more the share price went above the strike, the higher the profit. At a $200 share price, we'd be able to close the call and put at $10.81 and $0.78 for a total of $11.59, or a total profit of $397.

If instead, the share price dropped below the strike price, we'd be in a similar situation but making money from the put. If it dropped $10 below the strike price at 14 days, then the call would be $0.67, and the put would be $10.65, nearly in reverse to the situation of a $200 share price.

If the stock stays close to the strike price, you'd be faced with selling the options at a near break-even price or at a loss. Waiting until close to the expiration date can ensure losses. Maximum loss is the amount spent to purchase the options.

These results indicate that for a straddle, the more dramatic the move in stock price, the better the results, and the safest approach is to buy close at the money or close to at the money. You can buy slightly in the money for the call or put if you expect the stock price to rise or fall, using one of the options to mitigate possible losses if your speculation is wrong.

Strangle

A long strangle is also a method to mitigate risk by purchasing two options. In this case, we buy two options with different strike prices. The idea, in this case, is to be insensitive to the directional movement of the stock price. The options are purchased out of the money, so you want a low strike price for the put option and a high strike price for the call option.

Returning to the previous example, we again assume the share price is $190 a share with 30 days to expiration. Now we will purchase a call option that has a strike price of $195, and a put option with a strike price of $185, so both are out of the money. Since the options are out of the money, the initial investment is cheap, relatively speaking. The call option will cost $3.17, while the put option will cost $3.01, for a cost of $6.18 or $618 for the total investment.

For a strangle to be profitable, the stock will have to move even more than for a straddle.

At 16 days to expiration, suppose that the stock price has risen to $200. The call is now worth $6.97. The put is worth $0.25, for a total of $7.22. So you could sell both options to close your position, taking a profit of $129.

If instead, the stock price were to drop to $180, the call would only be worth $0.22, but the put would be worth $6.67, so your profit, in this case, would be $71.

A dramatic move can make this strategy very profitable. If instead, the share price dropped to $160, while the call would be virtually worthless, the put would shoot up to $24.98, for a total earning of $2,498, giving you substantial profits. A similar situation would happen in reverse for a dramatic move to the upside.

So the advantages of this strategy are that you profit no matter which way the share price moves, provided the move is large enough. However, the downside is your profits are limited unless there is a dramatic move in the share price. So if you are anticipating a large move in the stock price but aren't sure which direction it is going to go (such as with an earnings call), this could be a viable strategy.

Spreads

So far, we've been looking at strategies that anyone with a level 2 rating or above can implement. Even if you aren't explicitly approved for strangles and straddles, you can still implement them by manually buying the options.

Now we get into more advanced territory because these strategies require the sale of an option, and you have to get brokerage approval to sell options, even when they are part of a strategy like the one we are going to investigate here.

A spread is the simultaneous purchase and sale of options for the same underlying stock, but you buy and sell a put option and call or vice versa. They have different expiration dates and/or different strike prices, leading to many possibilities.

A vertical spread involves buying an option and selling an option but with different strike prices and the same expiration dates. The goal of a vertical spread is to limit risk and capital requirements. To sell a call, you either have to own 100 shares of stock or be able to purchase the shares, that is, have enough capital on hand to make the trade in the event the option was exercised, no matter how unlikely that may be.

Remember that you can take the examples to expiration, in which case out of the money options will expire worthlessly.

But for our example here, we will consider closing the position as well.

So let's take an example. You can use out of the money calls to do the spread. We can sell a call with a given strike price, and then buy another call that has a higher strike price. Suppose our stock is trading at $160 a share. We could sell a call with a strike price of $165 for $2.41. Then we could buy a call with a strike price of $175, for $0.53. The net credit to our account is given by the difference, and so is $2.41 - $0.53 = $1.88.

Now let's go to 15 days to expiration and look at three possible scenarios. The first scenario is when the stock prices rise substantially, so that both calls are in the money. So we'll pick a share price of $190.

In that case, the $175 call is worth $15.19, and the $165 call is worth $25.02. This is a bad situation since we sold the $165 call. There would be a risk it would be exercised, but we can use the following strategy which limits losses. First, we can sell the $175 call. Then we buy back the $165 call, and our total losses are limited to the difference, which is $9.83, so a total loss of $983. But remember the initial credit of $188 that helps mitigate the loss.

Suppose that we had sold the $165 call naked, without using a vertical spread. Then our total loss would have been $25.02 or $2,502. So we saved ourselves quite a bit on the loss.

Note that the difference in strike prices limits the losses in this case where the stock price rises above the higher strike price, to any value. So for this example, the losses are limited to $10. This is easy to see by plugging the numbers into an options calculator. You find that if the share price rises to $250, the $165 call is $85.02, but the $175 call would be $75.02. If the share price increased to $500, then the $175 call would be priced at $325 and the $165 call at $335.

So that is the power of this technique, the difference in the prices – and therefore, the maximum loss – is always the difference in the strike prices. So you can set your maximum loss by choosing your strike prices appropriately. Also don't forget that you can add in the initial credit, which for this example was $1.88 or a total of $188.

Now suppose that the share price goes between the two strike prices, so above $165 but less than $175. We will conveniently choose $170. In that case, the call option with the strike of $165 is worth $6.36. The $175 strike is worth $1.43. So our total loss would be $6.36 - $1.43 - $1.88 = $3.05. Again, the loss is limited.

Break-even is the price paid to enter the position plus the short strike price. In this example, that is $1.88 + $165 = $166.88. If the share price is below $166.88, then the spread will be profitable. Anywhere above this price, there will be losses, limited to the difference between the strike prices. Of course, you would choose a smaller range than the one selected here, which was for illustration.

So if the stock price dropped to $160, the option both options expire worthlessly, and we keep the premium.

To summarize:

Maximum profit is the credit you get for entering the vertical spread. That is the difference between the option you sell and the one you buy.

Maximum loss is the difference in strike prices minus the amount credited for entering the trade. In the example given, the difference in strike prices was $10, but the account was credited $1.88 for the spread, so the maximum loss is $10 - $1.88 = $8.12.

Capital requirement is equal to the maximum loss, so you need $812 to enter this trade, which is a lot lower than the capital requirement that would be required just selling a call.

A vertical spread allows you to enter a trade without predicting how the stock price will move.

The probability of profit is higher than the probability of loss, even though the potential magnitude of losses will be higher than the magnitude of profit.

Bull Call Spread

A bull call spread is a trade to enter when you believe that stock prices are going to increase by a small amount. Like the other strategies considered, losses are limited, but it also limits potential profits. Since you start off with a loss, it's called a debit spread.

This strategy involves buying and selling two call options with the same date of expiration but different strike prices. You buy a call option that is out of the money, and then sell a call option with a higher strike price (so it's also out of the money). Suppose that our stock was trading at $140 a share. We could buy a call option that has a $142 strike price with 30 days to expiration for $2.97. Then we could sell a call option that has a $144 strike price for $2.23. We start out at a loss of $0.74. If the share price rises to $145 by one day to expiration, the $142 call is worth $3.04, and we can sell it. The $144 call would be worth $1.33. We can buy it back, so our total profit would be $3.04 - $1.33 - $0.74 = $0.97 = $97.

If the stock price were to drop below the lower strike price, both options would expire worthlessly, and the total loss would be limited to the difference in option premiums paid to enter the position, which in this case would be $0.74.

The breakeven price is the strike price for the long call + net premiums paid. In this example, the call we purchased had a strike price of $142, and the total premium paid was $0.74, so the break-even price is $142.74. We make a profit for any share price that is higher than $142.74.

For example, if the share price is $143 at 1 day to expiration, the option we sold will expire worthlessly, but the option we purchased could be sold for $1.32. Subtracting the initial debit, the net profit is $1.32 - $0.74 = $0.91 for a total of $91.

Bear Call Spread

A bear call spread is a strategy using two call options when you expect a modest decrease in price. The two call options will have the same date of expiration but different strike prices. You sell a call with a lower strike price and buy a call with a higher strike price. The maximum profit is the net premium credited to your account, which is the premium of the lower strike price call you are paid less the premium you pay to purchase the higher price long call. The maximum loss is limited to the difference in the strike prices less the net premium paid.

Bull Put Spread

This is a credit spread involving two put options. Both put options will have the same expiration date. In this case, you sell a put option that has a given strike price and then buy a put option that has a lower strike price. In an opposite manner to a bull call spread, the profit is realized by a net credit received from the sale of the put option with the higher strike less the purchase of the second put option. This is the same for maximum loss; it is the result when the net credit from the sale and purchase of the puts is subtracted from the strike prices. This strategy seeks to profit from a small increase in share price over the lifetime of the option.

Bear Put Spread

A bear put spread seeks to profit from a modest decline in the share price. In this case, you buy and sell two puts with the same expiration date. You buy a put with a given strike price set to profit from a decline in stock price, and then sell a put with a lower strike price. This is a debit spread, so the sale of the put offsets the investment in buying the first put. In this case, the maximum loss is the net premium paid. So if you buy a put for $1, and sell a put for $0.75, the maximum loss is $0.25, or $25 in total. The maximum profit is the difference in the strike prices less the net premium paid.

Rolling Your Positions

You can "roll" your positions, which means buying and selling options at new expiration dates, to close and reopen your positions. This can be done if it appears a trade you've entered isn't going to work. Strike prices can be kept the same or modified. If you have a spread, you might change the range between the two strike prices. Rolling your positions might help you become profitable but can also result in increased losses. If you roll up, then you are rolling with an increase in strike prices, while roll down means rolling while decreasing strike prices. You could also "roll," that is close and reopen the positions, with longer expiration dates but the same strike prices.

Iron Condor

An iron condor is a strategy that is more advanced, with the hope that the stock price will stay within a range of share prices. You open an iron condor position by selling a call and a put option, with the call option having a relatively high strike price and the put option having a low strike price. For example, we could consider a stock with a share price of $100 at the time we open our position. If the recent history of the stock shows that the share price has been between $95 and $105, we could sell a call that has strike price of $105 and a put that has a strike price of $95. Then, the call would sell for $1, netting us $100. The put would sell for $88, so our total premium received would be $188. If the stock price stayed within the range, then both options would expire worthlessly, and we would pocket the premiums.

The iron condor has two more pieces, which are purchased for the sake of adding some insurance to the trade. Two calls are purchased that are further out of the money. That means you purchase a call that has a higher strike price than the strike used on the call option you sold, and you buy a put with a lower strike price than the strike used on the put you sold. In our example, we could buy a call that has a strike price of $110 and then buy a put that has a strike price of $90. Then, the put would cost $18, and the call would cost $28, so the net premium for the four options would be the total credits minus debits:

$188 - $18 -$28 = $142

If the price of the stock goes above the strike price we sold (in this example, $105) or below the strike price for the sold put (in this example, below 495), the trade could result in a loss. Maximum loss is differences between the strike prices minus the net credit from entering the position. Break-even points are the inside strike prices plus or minus premiums. So in this example, the lower breakeven point is $95 -$0.88 = $94.12 and the upper break-even point is $105+$1 = $106. If the stock price fails to fall within the range set by the sold call and put, the loss incurred would be from the sold put option which would be in the money. If the stock rises above the range set by the sold call and put, that is above upper range then there would be a loss from the in the money $105 call.

And again, if the share price stays within the range set by the strike prices of the sold call and put, then the profit would be realized because all four options expire worthlessly and the profit is the premiums earned less the money spent to buy the outside or range options.

An iron condor is an advanced trading strategy only open to level 3 or higher traders. It is used when you think the stock price will remain boxed in between two values over the lifetime of the option.

Butterfly Spreads

Butterfly spreads are another advanced trading technique, and again, they will have predictable but limited profits and limited losses. There are different types of butterfly spreads that depend on the expected volatility over the lifetime of the options. If volatility is low and not much change in stock price is expected, you can use a long butterfly spread. Two call options are purchased; one has a low strike price, and the other one has a high strike price. Then, two at the money call options are sold.

If high volatility is expected, that is your expectation is for significant changes in the stock price, and you can use a short call butterfly spread. The roles of long and short are switched; that is, you buy two call options that are close to or at the money and sell a call option with a low strike price and sell a call option with a high strike price.

In either case, the maximum loss is limited to the cost of setting up the butterfly spread. Maximum profits are limited to the premiums collected from selling the options less the premiums paid to buy the other options.

Adjusting a Butterfly to a Condor

The butterfly is adjusted to a condor by using both calls and puts, rather than all call options. They are different strategies for different situations.

Chapter 4 Types of Options

Options come in two major types – put options and call options. Traders choose the kind of option to trade-in depending on whether they want to buy or sell on the options market.

Call Options

The call option options make it possible for you to purchase an underlying asset associated with the option in question. When a call option is in the money, the bid or strike price is less in value than the underlying stock price. Traders always buy a call option when there is a possibility of its stock price to increase beyond the current bid price before the expiration is obtained. When this happens, the trader derives some profit from the call transaction.

Individuals who purchase call options are always known as holders. Once they acquire the option, they can sell it anytime before the expiration date. The profit of any option is obtained by subtracting the strike price, premium and transaction fees from the stock price. The resulting amount is what is called the intrinsic value. This difference is always a negative value when the trader has made a loss and zero value when no profit or loss has been realized.

The maximum amount that a trader can lose from an option is equivalent to its premium. This explains why most people purchase options and not the underlying security.

The call option comprises of three components-the strike price, the premium, and the exercise or expiration date. The premium is the amount of money that a trader pays when acquiring a particular option. For instance, a trader may purchase a call option with $55 as the strike price, $5 premium and an expiration period of one month; it means that you will pay the seller $5 as premium. If the expiration date is reached before you exercise the option, you will only pay the $5. If let's say, a week later the price goes up to $70 and you decide to sell your option, you will make a profit of $15 from the transaction less $5 paid as the premium. If the price goes below $55, you make a loss.

Investors may also decide to sell a call option when they are anticipating a decline in the stock price. As the stock price falls to a level that is lower than the strike price, the investor will get some profit from the transaction. The person selling a call is known as the writer of the call. He is one with the obligation to sell shares to a buyer at a price determined beforehand.

Put Options

This grants you the ability to write or sell an asset or security at a cost that is already predetermined, also the expiration date. Both call and put options can be used on stocks, commodities, currencies, and indexes as underlying securities. In this case, the strike price becomes the cost by which you sells the option.

A put option allows you to sell a certain asset at a known cost and expiration date. This option can be used on a good number of underlying assets including indexes, currencies, commodities, and stocks. The price at which a trader sells an option is called the strike price.

Traders make a profit from selling a put option when anticipating a decline in the strike price. They make a loss when the value of the stock increases to a level that is beyond the strike price. This indicates that the cost of a put option may rise or fall as time elapses.

A put option's intrinsic value can be derived by obtaining the difference in prices for the stock and the option. The resultant value keeps changing as the time value reduces in strength. When a stock option bears a positive intrinsic value, you say that it is in the money. A negative value of this shows that the option has fallen out of the money.

Similar to call options, you do not need to wait for your put options to expire before you exercise them. Since an option's premium value keeps varying with the stock price or the cost of any other underlying asset, it is important that you exercise your options just at the right time to avoid incurring losses in future.

Chapter 5 Intermediate Strategy – The Long Strangle

The other name for the long strangle is the "buy strangle" or just "strangle". It is a neutral strategy that requires the concurrent purchasing of a somewhat "out-of-the-money" call of the same expiration date and underlying stock. The objective is to benefit if the stock either goes up or down. Keep in mind though that purchasing both a put and a call adds to the price of your position, particularly for a volatile stock. This means that you will require a notable price swing just to break even. Both of these are volatile options strategies and should not be attempted by beginner. If you are to start with one option, start with a "long strangle".

This strategy is used when you believe the underlying stock will undergo noteworthy volatility in the near term. This means that you are sure that the underlying asset will change in value but not confident as to which direction. For example in our Trading Places example, the crop reports were known before their release allowing the good guys to pull ahead, but in a real world scenario these reports made public to everyone at the exact same time. They are read aloud on television to ensure the information is spread to everyone at the exact same time. In an event like this, or any other where the outcome is unknown, but it could have major changes on the price of a stock or commodity, a long straddle will help you get some profit. The one constant you need is to have a big swing on the product or stock.

This strategy has unlimited profit and limited risk. If the stock goes up, the potential profit is unlimited. The risk is if the underlying stock price is trading between the strike prices of the options bought on expiration date then maximum loss will unfortunately be reached. In this scenario you would lose the total initial debit acquired to begin the trade because both options would expire with no value. The potential loss, however, is slight because it is only the net debit paid for both options.

To initiate the strangle strategy, all you have to do is buy both an out of the money call option as well as an out of the money put option on the underlying asset. This allows you to earn whether the stock moves in either direction. The call option is for if the stock moves above the strike price and the put option is in case the stock moves lower than the strike price. On either option the profit is unlimited on both the upside and downside.

The Steady Stock

If you believe that a stock will remain steady, you can use call and puts to make money on the premiums collected. This requires you keep a long put position in an underlying asset while selling a call against that underlying asset.

This strategy is mostly used when someone holds the asset long and at the same time has a short position through the option to result in earnings from the option premium. You are essentially making money off of the stability of the stock price, but are hedging your bet in case the price rises. You have the prerogative, since you own stock, to sell this stock at any moment for the market price. This strategy is basically just trading this right to someone else for immediate cash. This could work well if the call option you are selling is valued less than your put option, and works especially well in cases where the stock remains at a steady price.

The advantage here is you are mitigating the risk of losing lots of money through the stock falling, and even though you are also sacrifices the potential to cash out when the stock reaches an unexpected high – this is still unexpected, and so you are really gaining short term cash in exchange for believing the stability of the stock price. At the same time, by having a long put on the same stock, you are enabling yourself to buy more stock if the price rises above the strike price. You are insuring yourself in all events, but this comes with a cost.

Sadly, the prospective earnings of this strategy is restricted since you had, in exchange for the premium, surrendered the possibility to entirely rake in the profits from a significant upward change in the cost of the underlying asset. Also you must watch out because you have to hang on to the shares for the whole time that you have the short hold option position, otherwise your asset will become a naked call. A naked call has limitless loss potential if the stock goes up. Once you enter these agreements you must remember that you obligated to complete them or risk great financial penalty.

Chapter 6 Intermediate Strategy – Bull Call Spread

The bull call spread is used when you believe that the value of a stock will rise reasonably in the near term. When using this strategy, you buy call options for a particular strike price but also sell the same number of calls of the identical expiration date and asset at a greater strike price. This is a vertical spread that comprises two calls with disparate strikes but the same expiration. The long call has a lower strike price than the short call meaning the bull call spread will necessitate an initial debit. The point of the short call is to aid in reimbursing the long call's initial cost.

The bull call spread is similar to the long call version but the compromise is that it has a capped upside potential. This is because even though the short call premium alleviates the total cost, it also caps off the potential profit. If you short the "out of the money" call you also cut down on the price for implementing your bullish position but the downside is that you are no longer able to make as much of a profit if the underlying asset price rises a lot. The total possible profit is the difference between the long option strike price and the short option strike price minus the net cost.

An example of when to use this strategy would be when you are hoping to take advantage of a growing stock while also not taking too much risk.

So how do you use this strategy? You need to buy an "at-the-money" call option but also write a greater striking "out-of-the-money" call option for the same expiration and same underlying security. You buy one call option and sell another.

Here is an example of a bull call spread: $18 dollars is the trading premium and you buy one call option with a strike price of $20 dollars as well as sell one call option with a strike price of $25 dollars. When the premium for the stock rises to $35, you have to give one hundred shares to the buyer of the short call for $25. This lets you purchase the shares at $20 but sell them for five dollars more instead of purchasing them at the market price $35 dollars and losing money on the trade.

This strategy can also be called the bull call debit because a debit is taken when beginning this trade.

Even though this strategy is more difficult than just purchasing a call, it can help decrease risk and set an objective for the cost depending on your outlook.

Chapter 7 Advanced Strategy – Modified Butterfly Spread

The regular butterfly spread comprises purchasing an "in the money" call option and selling two "at the money" call options while also purchasing another "out of the money" call option. This can also be done the same way with put options. Puts are meant to set up a bullish trade while call set up a bearish trade. This neutral strategy is a merger of the bear spread and bull spread.

As opposed to a regular butterfly that has two breakeven costs and fluctuation in the earnings potential, this strategy has a single breakeven cost and it is usually "out of the money." The point of this strategy is to make a profit even when the underlying security does not go beyond a specific price range.

To enter this strategy you have to first purchase one "out of the money" put option, then sell three puts at a lower strike price and finally purchase two puts at an even more reduced strike price. The modified call butterfly would be done exactly like this but with call options instead of put options. Try to enter this strategy between four and six weeks before expiration.

The modified butterfly strategy has limited profit but on the upside also has limited risk. The downside is however, that the comparison of profit potential to risk potential is not good. The normal, unchanged butterfly has a good reward to risk ratio but this altered strategy has a greater risk than maximum profit potential. When you are deciding whether to use this strategy, please contemplate the risk, the return and the probability of profit. This strategy is good for you if you have an appreciation for the butterfly but would like a little more flexibility. You should only use the modified butterfly if you are the type of trader who stays watchful of the stock and are able to adjust when needed. If you are, you will be able to find many great situations for the modified butterfly. This is not the type of strategy that you set and then forget. You need to be ready to react and have a plan for if your underlying security starts to drop, notably when it arrives at the breakeven price.

If the underlying security goes beyond the specific price range, either up or down, your strategy has failed. If you enter this strategy appropriately, however, the underlying security would have to make a big jump for you to attain maximum loss. Your intention with this strategy is for the underlying security to not drop discernibly. For example dropping a small amount or staying the same would be great. This way we can keep the premium we received when entering that trade. This is how you make the most profit but you can still make a smaller amount if the stock goes up. Your hope is that the stock will not decrease sharply.

Chapter 8 The Best 3 Ways to Improve Your Options Trading Education

here are a few different ways to expand your options trading training. The vast majority of them permanently require your time and may not cost any cash forthright. While there are a lot of different techniques for finding out about options trading, here are three ordinarily utilized chances.

Coach - Starting an association with an options broker as your tutor is likely the ideal approach to learn. There is nothing superior to anything utilizing genuine models as a significant aspect of your options trading instruction. Books, distributions, and other hard copy materials can offer excellent material - however, nothing looks at to first-hand involvement. Having a tutor will give you an unmistakable preferred standpoint over your opposition.

Mimicked Trades - If you have a record with an online intermediary, at that point you may as of now put reenacted options exchanges. This can be an incredible learning instrument for those hoping to build their options trading instruction. Purchasing and selling options through mimicked exchanges is first-hand knowledge of how the general financial exchange functions, without the danger of losing real cash.

Books and Publications - While not the cheapest option, utilizing magazines or different productions to expand your online options training works very well for certain financial specialists. You may likewise hope to agree to accept part sites or expect to minimal effort eBooks to facilitate your instruction. Do whatever it takes not to spend a great deal of cash on these as you can most likely discover a ton of free data too.

Regardless of whether you are finding out about selling secured calls, purchasing and selling somewhere down in the cash calls, or finding out about investment opportunity cites - instructing yourself is a significant advance in turning into a fruitful dealer.

Trading Education is the Key

Likewise, with anything throughout everyday life, training is vital for progress. If you know, at that point you can do anything you set your brain to. This incorporates online options trading just as turning into a savvy speculator of the financial exchange. If you are fueled with the correct data and can gain from your oversights, there is no determining what sort of financial specialist you can be!

For extra data on Options Trading appeal, look at - Options Income System for more subtleties.

Adapt precisely how to make a month to month pay, rake in huge profits in the market whether it goes up or down, day exchange with certainty and significantly more...

Financial Derivatives - Why Trading Simulators Are the Fastest and Best Way to Learn

There are not many, in any, pragmatic aptitudes that are procured by hypothetical learning alone. Trading financial derivatives are, in such manner, unquestionably not an exemption to the standard. But when the vast majority who are new to derivatives, regardless of whether they are student traders in speculation banks or private people, first methodology trading such items, they submerge themselves in books about the hypothesis, arithmetic and demonstrating.

In endeavoring to secure different abilities, no less specialized, practice is given need over hypothesis in pretty much every case. In the case of learning to play the violin or how to direct relevant examinations, any art is best learned by doing. Unquestionably, the hypothesis has its place. Without some primary direction, what other site does somebody start? It is each of the issues of equalization. Furthermore, as for learning how to trade financial derivatives, typically things are out of kilter. As of not long ago, it has all been hypothesis, and next to no training.

So why has this been the situation? There is a particular reason why people new to financial derivatives, regardless of whether they intend to trade, oversee hazard or need to comprehend them for expert purposes, give the excessive load to hypothesis overtraining. Also, that is the trouble in finding a reasonable preparing condition. The financial markets themselves are probably going to make for expensive teachers. Given the hazardous idea of derivatives, missteps can be costly. However, when learning any new expertise, it is through the very demonstration of committing errors that one learns and, from that point, improves. In the case of learning how to drive or how to explain complicated conditions, committing mistakes along the way is an essential piece of the learning procedure.

With regards to financial derivatives, this way has up to this point not been available. Since derivatives are, by their tendency, more convoluted than straightforward stocks and offers, the chance to work on trading in a reproduced domain has not existed until in all respects as of late. Luckily, this circumstance is presently changing, and another age of online derivatives trading simulators are developing. These offer clients the chance to learn how derivatives work through realistic practice sessions, intelligent assistance systems and point by point investigation of the client's presentation. Furthermore, instead of just focusing on the essential, directional properties of derivatives, the new advances teach clients how financial derivatives work in full. This enables clients to encounter derivatives trading, with all the related dangers and openings, in a totally chance free condition., before they adventure into the live markets.

Such innovation is the front line. It offers critical focal points over the old methods for learning how derivatives work and trade, and for anybody either planning to ace derivatives trading or merely searching for an underlying knowledge, it gives a vital learning device.

Dependable guideline: The Do's and Don'ts of Options Trading

There are many dependable guidelines to pursue as a starting trader, and this part will break down a portion of the do's and don'ts of options trading.

Try not to assess the situation and option trading tips. Mainly as a beginner trader, once people comprehend what you accomplish professionally, you'll likely get a wide range of stock and option trading tips from companions, family, colleagues, maybe even outsiders who just met you. A tipster will prescribe a stock dependent on some "insider data" concerning an organization or a commodity, however trading dependent on stock tips can devastate your record.

Without incorporating some trading procedure in their proposal, the tipster could be setting you up for disappointment. Tuning in to tips is OK, yet regardless you have to play out your own very prepared, exceedingly talented due persistence for any stock or options trade. You have to answer the "who, what, where, when, and why" of that trade.

Along with these similar rules of due persistence, here's another tip: never get into a trade except if you realize the amount you're willing to lose versus what you hope to make.

Do deal with your money well. You need to ensure that you are rehearsing legitimate money the executive's abilities. Ensure that before you put a trade on, you have built up a familiar object. Notwithstanding the tremendousness or vacancy of your wealth and the rule measure of money you're contributing, never sink over 10% of your portfolio in one trade, one stock, one option, or one division.

One rule to pursue is the standard of ten. Put 10% of each trade you make into one stock or options, and attempt to have 8-10 positions on the double. That way, in case you're in ten distinct areas, and one loses money in your record, and it's easy for you to dump and you're not leaving the business.

Also, that raises another "do." You need to treat your trading vocation as a business. If you have ten workers, and you have one terrible seed, you must cut the string. The equivalent goes for trading. You must dispose of that trade that is costing you money and assets and discover a substitution.

Do work on trading with a phony record before you dispatch a real existence, money subsidized trading or broker record. There are many excellent trading simulators available, many of them through whatever broker you choose to trade with. There are likewise a lot of programming organizations out there that have great phony trading stages available for buy and download. You can rehearse, similarly as though you're trading real money, consistently until you become active and agreeable in your new trading skin.

When you can't profit in a trading test system, at that point you're tricking yourself if you believe you're going to benefit in a subsidized, live trading record.

Make trade money that you can bear to lose, and don't contact any cash you can't. Try not to utilize the $10,000 charge card limit you're endorsed for to take out a $5,000 loan credit to subsidize your trading business. You can't bear to lose that money. What's "reasonable" is diverse for everybody, so you need to take a cold, hard item take a gander at your startup capital you plan to distribute to your trading business. Be sincerely and financially arranged to lose everything - because it can occur.

You've settled on a great decision in choosing that trading for dynamic and automated revenue is the right business move for you, and stocks, options, and other open, open financial markets are an excellent method to arrive. With Invest to Success' 10 Steps to Trading Success, you will learn how to position yourself to make every day, week after week reliably, and monthly profits for your portfolio with insignificant hazard, regardless of whether you're pristine to trading or a seasoned star!

How to Become a Top Option Trading Expert

Trading investment opportunities, when contrasted and regular stock trading, has numerous points of interest. Much the same as different sorts of contributing, it is fundamentally essential to have an adequate measure of information about the kind of speculations before setting out on this endeavor.

Online Stock Options trading has turned out to be a standout amongst the best ventures which have exploited the increasing velocity and accessibility of the web. The sheer volume of online trade has abandoned conventional brokers sheer volume of online business has left regular brokers, and options trading has turned out to be accessible to an extensive global network, who presently take an interest in the broad US market quickly.

If you have next to no learning about investment opportunities, it is fundamental that you do your research before beginning. Read a book or go to classes. Investment opportunities have different kinds of trading, buying and selling accessible and can in this manner be entangled. Make sure of the types of options you need to attempt and research the particular area. Realize the trading terms; a large number of which are recorded underneath.

Calls

Puts

Long and short call

Long and short put

Long and short engineered

Get back to and set back spread

Call-bull and put-bull spread

Secured call

Defensive put

Neckline

Call-bear and put-bear spread

A long and short straddle

Short and Long guts

Put-time and Call-time spread.

Call-proportion and put-apportion vertical

Short-call and Long-call butterfly

Long-put and short-put butterfly

Long and short condor

Know at any rate the essential meanings of these terms.

Make certain to make sure to use the broad assets accessible on the web and buy into the different bulletins for investment opportunities trading. Become an individual from gatherings and be present on options trading news. Make it your propensity to every day read what's happening in the market.

A decent method to begin your raid into trading is to try out a course, system or use instructional exercises. Many free instructional practices are offered online that will give you the fundamentals of investment opportunities and trading. A portion of these instructional exercises have recordings, precedents and other intuitive materials which will demonstrate value to new to trading investment opportunities. An assortment of on the web and disconnected courses are likewise accessible and may incorporate eBooks, gatherings, participation, spreadsheets, recordings, sound documents, DVDs and different materials. Courses uniquely intended to train you on the most proficient method to trade can be precious to option trading novice.

In conclusion, there are various programming systems and bundles for options trading that can assist you with analyzing and mimic situations in options trading and can be essential devices in your investment opportunities trading.

Forex Trading - Says Who?

When you are hoping to buy an eBook about profiting in the forex trading market, you need to pose one inquiry before giving out your charge card subtleties: who are you getting your trading counsel from? The nature of your forex instruction is just comparable to the individual or the people you are learning from. When you are getting your information and learning procedures from individuals who have not traded the systems that they are teaching, much stays to be found regarding their accomplishment in actual trading. The reason they are selling you these trading items may very well be because that is the leading way they can profit - just by selling and not by real trading.

You can check the veracity of these promoting claims by requesting a real-time track record that has been reviewed and demonstrated to have been utilized in real trading. Search for a reputation of around a few years. As a rule, you won't get any just because there aren't any as the majority of these have not been traded. The more significant part of these digital books depends on reenacted and ideal situations with shutting costs that are already known to the trader. Along these lines, while their trades may work in their recreations, there is no assurance that they will work in real trades. Reenactments are unquestionably unique about actual trades.

Just trust forex trading experts who have astounding trading track records in having the option to round up benefits over the long term. These experts recognize what they are discussing and are sharing learnings from their encounters and not from minor suppositions. Information about forex trading can be researched on the web. Ensure you approve and check your information diligently to guarantee that you are learning the correct exercises and systems for fruitful forex trading.

Forex Options Trading - In the World of FOREX Trading

In the Forex World, Forex is the most significant budgetary Foreign Exchange market on the planet. Not quite the same as other markets like stocks or item, The Forex open 24hours, Monday to Friday 24/5 week by week. What's more, it has a normal of 3.2 Trillion trade ordinary. Concerning now, it is an excellent time to go into Forex market because of a terrible economy, concerning the stock and ware are bearish yet the US Dollar is bullish. This will in general lead to an extremely fluid market and is an alluring market to trade.

The FX market does not have a fixed exchange. It is traded through banks, brokers, dealers, money related organizations and private people. Trades are executed through telephone and increasingly through the Internet. It is just over the most recent couple of years that the smaller investor has had the option to access this market. Already, a lot of stores required blocked the smaller investors. With the approach of the Internet and developing a challenge, it is currently easily in the reach of general investors.

With the development system nowadays, you can trade the Forex market with as low as US$200 with an influence proportion of 1-200. Indeed, even with a democratic administration of market diagramming data, updates and news. That is the reason nowadays there's increasingly more exchange in the Forex market. The market additionally turned out to be fluid likewise because of little investor that came in, an amount which changes the market condition.

As should be evident that individual is acquainted with the energizing universe of Forex Trading from various perspectives: companions, recent developments, papers, TV, and numerous others. For many of you who are new to Forex, the accompanying rules spread the nuts and bolts of currency trading. You even can begin which a demo account which is a recreation of the live trading record information feed. The Broker will enable you to preliminary out utilizing a reenactment of $100,000 virtual money to trade live market.

In Forex Market, there's dependably chance... So a Stop-Loss is dependably an absolute necessity in forex trading. With the sound system and order, you will find accomplishment in Forex Trading. Trading is a mind diversion; you should change your mental attitude first from a typical individual to that of a theorist. Practically all traders I have met, with the exception of a couple of fruitful ones who really made billions trading in the market, basically squander all their time attempting to learn the most natural part in flawlessness, as about how to read information and diagrams, and endeavoring to consummate passage and leave aptitudes, and so forth. Trading is a mind diversion, and without having a correct attitude, it is a losing amusement even before it begins. Preparing a trader's brain is the first step for any fruitful trader yet practically all new traders disregard that part, and that clarifies why over 95% of traders are a disappointment over the long haul.

Chapter 9 Options Trading Simulator

There is a close link between stock trading and options trading. However, options are not the same as stocks. Options are largely used to generate a profit using much smaller investments compared to stock investments. Another use of options is to insure against losses.

There are quite a number of reputable simulators online and one of the most reliable and trusted one is the simulator from Investopedia. This firm is not only the leading financial information and services firm but has an amazing wealth of resources online. The simulator uses actual data from stock markets so as to produce real life experience of using a real brokerage account.

Introduction to the trade simulator

The trade simulator is used for a number of reasons by different people. For instance, instructors use it as an instrument to teach their students all about the stock and options markets and how to use it. Some people use this simulator to try out new trading strategies while others just use it to find out what the real trading account feels like. Basically, the main purpose of the simulator is to simply make you, or any other user, a better trader.

There are a couple of tabs located on the top side of the user interface. With each of these tabs, a user will have the chance and ability to navigate through the system and all the different sections of the simulator. When you click any of these tabs, then more links will appear and these will offer you more choices. Here is a look at the 7 separate tabs found on the online trading simulator.

Tabs on the trading simulator

Home: The home button takes you to the home page and gives you an overall outlook of your trading account. Here, you are able to access other tabs and get to the pages you desire. At the home page, you also get an opportunity to change your settings and profile.

Portfolio tab: This particular tab provides users with a summary of the stocks, shares, options and all other holdings.

Watch list tab: This particular tab enables you to easily and efficiently track any stocks you want but without allocating any cash to any part of the portfolio. It is easy to add new stocks and manage the current ones from here.

Stock research: The stock research tab comes with important tools that enable users to carry out research on the performance of stocks and of companies that they may be interested in. Some of the tools available include a ticker lookup tool, a research tool and so much more.

The trading tab: This tab contains the section of the simulator where users get to enter or input their trade orders. They are also able to review all open, failed and outstanding trades.

Ranking tab: Another tab you will notice on the options trading tab is the ranking tab. This is an important tab that instantly lets you know of your current placing enabling you to opt for any specific competition.

Messages tab: This is a tab that allows users to check your messages that are in your inbox. There will sometimes be messages sent to you and users will also be able to send messages to others.

Games tab: There is a games tab on the trade simulator that allows any user to manage, review and create games. You will find active games which you can join and participate in. users are by default invited to join in some games and the choice to join in or not is voluntarily made.

Awards: Any user who successfully completes different trade simulator activities, especially trade activities gets to receive an award.

Help: It is always good to know that help is at hand whenever needed. As a trader and investor, if you ever need help with tutorials or have any general questions, then you simply need to click this tab.

Using the simulator to place orders and buy stock options

You are now familiar with the tabs on the trade simulator and can use these buttons at any stage of trade. The next step now is to set up and submit a trade using this simulator. We will now endeavor to purchase 100 shares of Walmart Stores Inc, abbreviated as WMT.

First, choose the trade tab and then enter WMT and 100. Figure 100 is entered in the quantity field while WMT is entered in the symbol field. The transaction needed is "Buy" while the price selected is market. The simulator will require a duration period and here you choose "Good Till Canceled".

Now select the Preview Order so as to view the order confirmation. The Preview Order will show the stock purchased, the type of trade, price and many other essential details that you need to trade successfully.

Please take a minute and confirm each and every detail on this preview. Ensure that all the details match what your trade details are. This is indeed a confirmation process, that you are buying 100 shares of Walmart Stores, abbreviated

WMT at market rates. For a real trade online, you would be charged a commission fee of about $20. Brokerage firms will charge you a commission for executing the trades on your behalf.

As soon as you confirm all the details on the Preview Page are, you may then proceed to submit the page. This will confirm your purchase of 100 shares of WMT at current market price. The order will now be filled when the next available opportunity presents itself. Should an order be placed outside of regular working hours, then the order will be executed first thing on the next trading day. Your order can be confirmed by checking out the order submission page. The stock simulator will confirm this for you.

The simulator will also indicate the stocks with the biggest gains on that particular day and those with the biggest losses. This is important information that can help and guide traders on how to place their trades.

If you check out your portfolio page, it should now indicate 100 shares of WMT as well as some cash balance. Now here is what the various items on the portfolio page mean.

Buying power: This refers to your capacity to buy options or shares and to trade. The buying power is typically based on your portfolio's value as well as cash amount. It is not possible to make trades that do exceed your indicated buying power.

Account value: This value means the total value of the portfolio as of that particular moment. This value is updated each night once the markets close. The currency of the account is also indicated in brackets.

Annual return: This term on your purchase page refers to the total returns, as a percentage, if all your annual returns were to be extrapolated for a given year.

Cash: Here, the amount of cash that you have in your account at the given moment will be displayed. The buying power display is considered a better indicator of financial position.

You will note that the account on the simulator is divided into 3 distinct parts. These are the option portfolio, the stock portfolio, and the shorted stock portfolio. The stock portfolio will indicate all the stocks that you currently have. It will indicate all the different values such as company name, the number of shares and so on.

It is important to learn how to interpret the Portfolio Summary page, it is important to now apply all these tools and ensure that you conduct trades as required. Let us now learn something else on the simulator.

Use of ticker symbol on the simulator

Even as you purchase stocks and options on the simulator, you may have noticed the system requesting a company's stock symbol in order to place a trade. Each company that joins the markets receives a unique stock symbol. Once the symbol is awarded, it will be unique to the company and none other can use this symbol.

The ticker symbol is sometimes chosen by the company itself or the bourse. It can be as brief as one single letter or as long as 5 letters. For instance, Ford Motor Company uses the letter F as its symbol

Ticker symbols

In many instances, news reports often quote companies using their initials which may confuse others to think of the initials as the ticker symbol. For instance, many newspapers across America often refer to the company Hewlett Packard as HP yet the company is quoted on the bourse as HPQ. This shows the need and importance of confirming a company's denotation or ticker symbol before entering any trades.

Any time you wish to purchase shares, stocks or options and all other financial instruments quoted at the markets, make sure to check the ticker symbol. Do not make a guess or an assumption otherwise you may purchase the wrong stock. Fortunately, most brokerage firms allow you to look up ticker symbols with their accounts. The trade simulator provides the same tool to search for a company's ticker symbol.

How to research ticker symbols on the simulator

Now, try and search for the ticker symbols of companies such as Pier 1 Imports and Nike. First, you click on the symbol lookup tab. This tab is found when you click on the Stock Research tab. You will receive a prompt so proceed and enter the search term, Nike and click search or enter. You will be shown the symbol NKE and a confirmation of the company whose ticker this is.

Similarly, when you follow the same procedure to find the ticker symbol of Pier 1 Imports, then you will receive the ticker symbol PIR and a confirmation of the company's details. This shows how fast and easy it is to find a company's ticker symbol.

Diversify your portfolio with the simulator

As an investor and trader, you should always diversify your portfolio. If you do not and instead put all your funds in a single product, then you risk losing all your funds should things not work out with the trade. Simply put, you should always diversify your trades.

The best way to succeed is to purchase and build a diversified equity portfolio. However, you need to be smart when you diversify. For instance, if you choose to invest in McDonald's Corporation, you should avoid investing in another fast food chain.

The reason is that, if the fast food industry was affected, your investments as a whole would take a hit. You should, therefore, buy some McDonald's shares and then diversify into a different field, say energy sector. You can consider buying shares in ExxonMobil, for instance.

When making real life decisions, you need to take a more scientific approach. This means using a system that ensures you diversify your portfolio in the right manner.

The GICS or Global Industry Classification Standards is widely used by traders, investors and fund managers among many others to diversify their portfolios. This system splits the economy into 10 different sectors. These 10 sectors are listed below.

1. Energy

2. Financials

3. Materials

5. Industrials

6. Utilities

7. Information Technology

8. Telecoms

9. Consumer

10. Health Care

Let us assume you already own WMT, PIR and TLAB shares. This means you own shares of Walmart, Pier 1 Imports, and Tellabs. You, therefore, want to avoid buying shares or stocks in the Telecom or consumer discretionary sectors. However, you can still purchase stock from 8 sectors. With the simulator, you can use a stock screener to get a list of available stocks within a particular sector.

Simply get onto the simulator and run a stock screen for your preferred sector. Now proceed to check out which stocks meet your analysis requirements and also interest you. There is a lot more to portfolio diversification and all these cannot be summarized here. Traders and investors often consider many other factors when diversifying their investments.

For instance, in your analysis, you may want to find out energy stocks with the best P/E ratios. You may want to investigate whether there are any other factors that may affect a particular stock in the long and short term. You should, therefore, endeavor to learn a little bit more about portfolio diversification.

Selling stocks on the trade simulator

Once you build a diversified portfolio of securities, you are now ready to start entering trades and deals. Ideally, your stocks and shares will not have seen plenty of price changes yet. Most investors often sell their shares at least a couple of months after initial buying. Here is how to proceed once you desire to sell.

You first need to determine when the best time is to sell your stock. You will look at the stocks and then find out which ones have seen some movement and gained value. One of the stocks in your portfolio, say, GE or General Electric is good for sale.

You will choose the number of shares you want to sell and then go to order stock tab. Several prompts will appear and will require that you enter the necessary details of the sale. For instance, you will need to enter the stock symbol, which is GE in our case, specify the transaction, which is "sell" and then the quantity.

Once all the details are entered onto the relevant sections, confirm that everything is correct and then submit the sell order for execution. If the sale is submitted within ordinary working hours or market hours, then it will be executed at the beginning of the next trading day.

Advanced trade types on the trade simulator

The limit order

By definition, a limit order constitutes the instructions from you, the trader, to the broker to trade a defined number of securities of a particular company at any time the market price is lower or equal to a price that you specify. As an example, you may be in possession of the Walmart shares valued at $70.35 per share. You may choose to dispose of these shares as soon as they gain 20% in value or at least $10 per share.

Now instead of checking the market every day to observe the trends in order to sell, you can simply submit what is known as a simple limit sell order. This order will then be processed as soon as the set terms are met.

On the trade simulator, click on the Trade tab and a drop down menu with links will appear. Once it appears, you then go ahead to enter the trade instructions described above. The limit set order will then be set up as required. You will also need to set up other details such as the number of stocks to be sold and so on. Your broker will then execute the order as soon as the conditions set are met.

The terms for such an order are often known as Good Till Canceled which means the broker should execute the order unless it is canceled by a trader. This kind of tool is very important. The limit set order is useful anytime you wish to dispose of a stock under certain market conditions but are unable to regularly or frequently check the market for these conditions.

Limit buy orders

In a similar manner, you can place limit buy orders with your broker through the trade simulator. You can instruct your brokerage to place a buy order for stocks or shares when certain conditions are attained, such as the desired price. For instance, remember the WMT shares purchased earlier (Walmart shares). Now, these were purchased at a price of $70.35 per share. Now suppose this was a high price and we had options. We could have issued limit buy orders to the broker, for instance, to buy the shares at or below $65 per share. This is a price we believe is fair and anything above this price is not.

Stop order

A stop order is basically considered to be a dormant order until such a time the stock or share price drops to a certain given amount, known as the stop price. It is easy to enter such an order on the simulator. All you need to do is define the parameters of the order and then go to the Order Stock tab. Here you will need to enter the details of the order.

These details include the stock symbol, transaction type such as sell or buy, the number of shares and the intended stop price. You also need to specify the time duration, usually Good Till Canceled. The stop price could be something like 20% lower than the purchase price, for instance. It is a very convenient option that you have as a trader and which you can use to enhance your portfolio and position in the market.

Short selling

Most sellers cringe at the thought of a bear market because all shares tend to lose value and trend downwards. However, the technique of short selling enables you, the trader, to profit from a bearish market.

Basically, a short sell can be described as an order where you, the trader, sells borrowed securities while all the time anticipating a decline or drop in share price.

Short selling may not be the easiest technique to implement and so it is easier to demonstrate with an example. Imagine that Microsoft shares MSFT are highly priced and likely to lose value in the coming days. As a trader, you wish to benefit from this situation so what you have to do is short the MSFT shares.

Since you do not own the shares, you borrow from another trader who has possession of them. Your brokerage firm will find the shares for you. Once you have them, you sell them at the stock market.

Imagine you sell the shares at $60 and two weeks later, the shares drop to $50 per share. At this point in time, you purchase the shares back from the stock market and give them back to the broker. You will notice that in the process, you will make $10 per share, minus commissions and fees.

Using the simulator for short selling

Now if you were to use the simulator for the same transaction, you would be able to accomplish the same feat. First, go to the Trading screen. Suppose you want to sell your Microsoft shares. You will then enter the stock symbol on the first tab and then describe the transaction type. In our current case, the transaction is a short sell. Define the quantity being sold, usually 100 or in multiples of 100. You then describe the duration as Good Till Canceled.

Once all this information has been supplied, you simply proceed to enter the trade and wait for your brokerage to execute the trade. It is normally executed first thing on the morning of the next business day. The brokerage will receive this information and understand it just as you have entered it so always counter-check and be extra careful.

Trade options on the simulator

Placing trades in options is a lot more complicated as compared to trading shares and stocks on the trade simulator. The starting point is similar though as you begin on the Trading tab. Once you hit this button, select the options trade button and choose the stock symbol of the shares you wish to invest in.

For instance, if you want options based on Microsoft stock then choose MSFT then select the Get Quote button. In instances where you are unsure of the stock symbol then you should look it up using the links provided.

Option Chain

In order to proceed with your options trade via the simulator, you will need an option chain. This is essentially a table with all option calls and puts provided. The chain provides additional details about each option. For instance, you can find out the bid and ask prices, the volume available and so on. There are two distinct lists which are Put options and Call options.

Notice that when trading with options, some details are entered for you. These include the expiry date, ticker symbol and the type of option you are trading in. The additional variable that you will enter is the number of contracts.

Now take a look at the order, confirm all the details are correct and everything else is in order. Once you confirm this on the Preview Order page, you may enter the transaction so your brokerage firm executes it for you first thing on the next business day. Remember that options are purchased only in contracts and 1 contract option has 100 shares.

Options and the trade simulator

Remember that options are different from trading shares. Options give you rights but not obligation to buy or sell shares at a set price for a limited and predetermined period of time. Options are often used to insure a portfolio against losses due to stock market downward spiral.

Remember the initial portfolio of shares we purchased. It contained shares from Walt Disney, Apple Inc, ExxonMobil, 3M Company and Dave Buster Entertainment. An analysis of these stocks shows ExxonMobil shares, which are pretty costly, could lose value very easily in the coming weeks. To protect your portfolio from the risk of losses, you can buy options to hedge against the expected losses.

The best tool for this is a put option. This put option can be accessed and purchased by again using the Trade Options page. Once you get to this page, type in XOM, the ExxonMobil ticker symbol and then click on Get Quotes. You can click on the options with a preferred date such as August 2017 and so on. You will then easily view all the current XOM options with an expiry date on the third Friday of August.

The need to purchase the Put option in our case is to prevent drastic losses on our ExxonMobil shares in the coming weeks. On the Put options table, you can choose the preferred option with a strike price of, let's say $75.00. From the table, we note that the options contract have an asking price of $30.90 so you will be required to pay $30.90 for the contract where each contract has 100 options.

The options price is $80.50 per share at the moment based on the chart on our simulator. If all the details look great on the Preview Order page, you may submit the trade and then proceed to enter it so it is ready for the brokerage. This Exxon put option should be processed within 20 minutes if received on time. So now for the next 1 month, no matter what happens, your Exxon shares will always be at or above the price of $75 per share, regardless of what happens to the actual shares at the stock market.

The process of selling options takes on the same sequence of events as you would when selling shares and stocks.

Chapter 10 The Best Strategies to Make Money

Good strategies of any kind of options trading are the major key to any kind of success that is about to be unfolded in any activity. Strategies are normally laid in the trading plan and should be strictly implemented in every options trading move that is likely to be involved. Let us wholly venture into the best strategies so far in options trading.

Collars. The collar strategy is established by holding a number of shares of the underlying stock available in the market where protective puts are bought and the call options sold. In this kind of strategy, the options trader is likely to really protect his or her capital used in the trading activities rather than the idea of acquiring more money during trading. This kind is considered conservative and rather much more important in options trading.

Credit spreads. It is presumed that the biggest fear of most traders is a financial breakdown. In this side of strategy, the trader gets to sell one put and then buy another one.

Covered calls. Covered calls are a good kind of strategy where a particular trader sells the right for another trader to purchase his or her stock at some strike price and get to gain a good amount of cash. However, there is a specific time that this strategy should be utilized and in a case where the buyer fails to purchase some of the stock and the expiration date dawns, the contract becomes invalid right away.

Cash naked put. Cash naked put is a kind of strategy where the options trader gets to write at the money or out of the money during a particular trading activity and aligning some particular amount of money aside for the purpose of purchasing stock.

Long call strategy. This is the most basic strategy in options trading and the one that is quite easy to comprehend. In the long call strategy for options trading, aggressive option traders who happen to be bullish are pretty much involved. This implies that bullish options traders end up buying stock during the trading activities with the hope of it rising in the near future. The reward is unlimited in the long call strategy.

Short call option strategy. The short call strategy is the reverse of the long call one. Bearish kind of traders is so aggressive in the falling out of stock prices during trading in this kind of strategy. They decide to sell the call options available. This move is considered to be so risky by the experienced options traders believing that prices may drastically decide to rise once again. This significantly implies that large chunks of losses are likely to be incurred, leading to a real downfall of your trading structure and everything involved in it.

Long put option strategy. First things first, you should be contented that buying a put is the opposite of buying a call. So in this kind of strategy, when you become bearish, that is the moment you may purchase a put option. Put option puts the trader in a situation where he can sell his stock at a particular period of time before the expiration date is reached. This strategy exposes the trader to a mere kind of risk in the options trading market.

Trading time. It is depicted that options trading for a longer period is much value as compared to a short period dating. The longer the trading day, the more skills and knowledge the trader is likely to be engaged into as he or she is likely to get the adequate experience that is needed for good trading. Mastering good trading moves for a while gives the trader the experience and adequate skills.

Bull call spread strategy. In this kind of strategy, the investor gets to purchase several calls at a particular strike price and then purchases the price at a much higher price. The calls always bear a similar expiration date and come from the same underlying stock. This type of strategy is mostly implemented by the bullish options traders.

Bear put strategy. This strategy involves a trader purchasing put options at a particular price amount and later selling off at a lower price amount. These options bear a similar expiration date and from the same underlying stock. This strategy is mostly utilized by traders who are said to be bearish. The consequences are limited losses and limited gains.

Iron condor. The iron condor involves the bull call spread strategy and the bear put strategy all at the same time during a particular trading period. The expiration dates of the stock are still similar and are of the same underlying stock. Most traders get to use this strategy when the market is expected to experience low volatility rates and with the expectation of gaining a little amount of premium. Iron condor works in both up and down markets are is really believed to be economical during the up and down markets.

Married put strategy. On this end, the options trader purchase options at a particular amount of money and at the same time, get to buy the same number of shares of the underlying stock. This kind of strategy is also known as the protective put. This is also a bearish kind of options trading strategy.

Cash covered put strategy. Here, one or more contracts are sold with a 100 shares multiplied with the strike price amount for every particular contract involved in the options trading. Most traders use this strategy to acquire an extra amount of premium on a specific stock they would wish to purchase.

Long or short calendar spread strategy. This is a tricky type of strategy. The market stock is said to be stagnant, not moving and waiting for the right timing until the expiration of the front-month is reached.

Synthetic long arbitrage strategy. Most traders take advantage of this strategy when they are trying to take advantage of the different market prices in different kinds of markets with just the same property.

Put ratio back spread strategy. This is a bearish type of options strategy where the trader gets to sell some put options and gets to purchase more options of just the same underlying stock with a similar expiration date and a lower price.

Call ratio back spread. In this strategy, the trader uses both the long and short options positions so as to eradicate consistent losses and target achieving large loads of benefits over a particular trading period. The essence of this strategy is to generate profits in case the stock prices tend to elevate and reduce the number of risks likely to be involved. This strategy is mostly implemented by bullish kind of options traders.

Long butterfly strategy. This strategy involves three parts where one put option is purchased at particular and then selling the other two options at a price lower than the buying price and purchasing one put at even lower price during a particular trading period.

Short butterfly strategy. In this strategy, three parts are still involved where a put option is sold at a much higher price and two puts are then purchased at a lower price than the purchase price and a put option is later on sold at a much lower strike price. In both cases, all put bear the same expiration date and the strike prices are normally equidistant as revealed in various options trading charts. A short butterfly strategy is the reverse way of the long butterfly strategy.

Long straddle. The long straddle is also known as the buy strangle where a slight pull and a slight call are purchased during a particular period before the expiration date reaches. The importance of this strategy is that the trader bears a large chance of acquiring good amounts of profits during his or her trading time before the expiration date is achieved.

Short straddle. In this kind of strategy, the trader sells both the call and put options at a similar price and bearing the same expiration date. Traders practice this strategy with the hope of acquiring good amounts of profits and experience limited various kinds of risks.

Owning positions that are already in a portfolio. Most traders prefer purchasing and selling various options that already hedge existing positions. This kind of strategy method is believed to incur good profits and incur losses too in other occurrences.

Albatross trade strategy. This kind of strategy aims at gaining some amounts of profits when the market is stagnant during a specific options trading period or a pre-determined period of time. This kind of strategy is similar to the short gut strategy.

Reverse iron condor strategy. This kind of strategy focuses on benefiting some profits when the underlying stock in the current market dares to make some sharp market trade moves in either direction. Eventually, a limited amount of risks are experienced and a limited amount of profits during trading.

Iron butterfly spread. Buying and holding four different options in the market at three different market prices is involved in the trading market for a particular trading period.

Short bull ratio strategy. Short bull ratio strategy is used to benefit from the amounts of profits gained from increasing security involved in the trading market in a similar way in which we normally get to buy calls during a particular period.

Bull condor spread. This is a type of strategy that is designed to return a profit if the actual price of security decides to rise to a predicted price range during a specific trading period impacting good chunks of profits made to the options trader and a limited number of risks involved.

Put ratio spread strategy. This strategy entails purchasing a number of put options and adding more options with various strike prices and equal kind of underlying stock during a particular options trading period.

Strap straddle strategy. Strap straddle strategy uses one put and two calls bearing a similar strike price and with an equal date of expiration and also containing the same underlying stock that is normally stagnant during a particular trading period. The trader utilizes this type of strategy for the hope of getting higher amounts of profits as compared to the regular straddle strategy over a particular period of the trading period.

Strap strangle strategy. This strategy is bullish, where more call options are purchased as compared to the put options and a bullish inclination is then depicted in various trading charts information.

Put back spread strategy. This back spread strategy combines both the short puts and long puts so as to establish a position where the ratio of losses and profits entirely depends on the ratio of their two puts that are likely to be experienced in the market.

Short call ratio. This strategy involves purchasing a single call and later on selling two other calls at a higher price amount during a specific period of time before its expiration. This concept combines the protocols of the bull call spread strategy and the naked call strategy. The essence of this strategy is to acquire limited loss potential and mixed profits potential to the options trader involved during a particular period of time.

Iron albatross strategy. The particular trader gets to use this type of strategy when expecting a particular underlying stock to trade during a particular period of time before expiration. Four transactions are usually involved in this strategy and a high level of trading is called for. This implies that this measure kind is so suitable for the experienced traders, ones who have mastered almost every market move.

Bull call ladder spread strategy. This one is almost similar to the bull call strategy where security increasing in price is expected to source out some profits to the trader during options trading.

Conclusion

Inexperienced traders are often warned away from purchasing options that are out of the money as being a greater risk than the ultimate reward is likely to be. While it is true that a short expiration time coupled with an out of the money option will frequently look appealing, especially to those with a smaller amount of trading capital to work with, the issue is that all of these types of options are likely to look equally appealing which leaves them with no way to tell the good from the bad. As a more experienced trader, however, you have many more tools at your disposal than the average novice which means that, while risky, cheap options have the potential to generate substantial returns, as long as you keep the following in mind while trading them.

Mishandling early assignment: Early assignment occurs when a holder exercises an option that you are the writer upon much early that you had anticipated, and at terms that are much less favorable than you had initially hoped. If this happens, it can be easy to become flustered and simply sell as requested, taking a loss in the process. Instead, it is important to consider all the possible options, including purchasing another option for the express purpose of selling it, to ensure that you mitigate the extra costs as completely as possible.

Ignoring the statistics behind options trading: One of the biggest mistakes that most newbie options traders make is that they forget the probability is a real thing. When you check a potential stock before purchasing an option, it's important to understand that the history of an option is important when deciding whether or not you should be investing in it, but so are the odds and probability surrounding whether or not a particular event is going to occur.

For example, a common strategy that investors use is to leverage their money by investing in cheap options so that this will help to prevent big losses on a stock that they actually own shares of. Of course, this is a good strategy, but nothing works one-hundred percent of the time. Make sure that if the rules of probability and simple ratios are telling you to stay away from a deal, you listen to the facts that are staring you in the face. Wishful thinking will come to bite you later on.

Being overzealous: Oftentimes when new options traders finally get their initial plan just right, they become overzealous and start committing to larger trades than they can realistically afford to recover from if things go poorly. It is important to take it slow when it comes to building your rate of return and never bet more than you can afford to lose.

Regardless of how promising a specific trade might seem, there is not risk/reward level at which it is worth considering a loss that will take you out of the game completely for an extended period of time. Trade reasonably and trade regularly and you will see greater results in the long term guaranteed.

Not being adaptable: The successful options trades know when to follow their plans but they also know that no plan will be the right choice, even if early indicators say otherwise. There is a difference between making a point of sticking to a plan and following it blindly and knowing which is which one of the more important indicators of the separation is between options trading success and abject failure. This means it is important to be aware of when and where experimentation and new ideas are appropriate and when it is best to toe the line and gather more data in order to make a well-reasoned decision.

This also means having several different plans in your options trading tool box and not just resolutely sticking to the first one that brings you a modicum of success. This is crucial as there are certain plans that will only work in specific situations and knowing which to use when, in real time, will lead to significantly greater returns on a more reliable basis every single time.

Likewise, an adaptive options trader knows that market conditions can change unexpectedly and is prepared to respond accordingly. This means understanding when the time is right to go in a new direction, regardless of the potential risks that doing so might entail. Sometimes a good trader has to make a leap of faith, and a trader who is successful in the long term knows what signs to look for that indicate this type of scenario is occurring in real time. Unfortunately, this type of foresight cannot be taught, and instead must be found with experience.

As long as you keep the appropriate mindset regarding individual trades, any new strategy that is attempted will result in valuable data, if nothing else. It is important to understand that learning not to use a specific course of action a second time is always valuable, no matter the costs.

Ignoring the probability: Always remember that the historical data will not apply to the current trends in the market at all times which means you will always want to consider the probability as well as the odds that the market is going to behave the way it typically does. The odds are how likely the market is to behave as expected and the probability is the ratio of the likelihood of a given outcome. Understanding the probability of certain outcomes can make it easy to purchase the proper options to minimize losses related to holdings of specific underlying stocks. When purchasing cheap options, it is important to remember that they are always going to be cheap for a reason as price is determined by strike price of the underlying stock as well as the amount of time remaining for the option to regain its value, choose wisely otherwise you are doing little more than gambling and there are certainly better ways to gamble than via options trading.

Letting the opinions of other influence your trading: While every day trader is going to have opinions regarding the best way to trade this type of stock or when to use that indicator, the best day traders tend to avoid this advice like the plague and instead work out their own. The only thing you really need to focus on in order to make the right types of trades in the right timeframes is math and anything else is only going to get in the way. Keep in mind that you want to analyze and observe economic and political events not get caught up in them.

Not dealing with short options properly: While, in theory, it might seem like buying back short options at the last moment is the best choice, this practice is sure to hurt your more than help you in the long run. It may be tempting to hold onto profitable options in order to squeeze the maximum return out of each investment but you need to be aware that the potential for a reversal is always lurking in the shadows. Instead, a good rule of thumb is to buy back options that are currently at 80 percent of your ideal return or higher and let the extra take care of itself. While it may hurt to leave some potential profit on the table, it will improve your overall reliability, netting you a profit in the long run.

Not considering exotic options: An exotic option is one that has a basic structure that differs from either European or American options when it comes to the how and when of how the payout will be provided or how the option relates to the underlying asset in question. Additionally, the number of potential underlying assets is going to be much more varied and can include things like what the weather is like or how much rainfall a given area has experienced. Due to the customization options and the complexity of exotic options, they are only traded over-the-counter.

While they are undoubtedly more complex to get involved with, exotic options also offer up several additional advantages when compared to common options including:

• They are a better choice for those with very specific needs when it comes to risk management.

• They offer up a variety of unique risk dimensions when it comes to both management and trading.

- They offer a far larger range of potential investments that can more easily meet a diverse number of portfolio needs.

- They are often cheaper than traditional options.

They also have additional drawbacks, the biggest of which is that they cannot often be priced correctly using standard pricing formulas. This may work as a benefit instead of a drawback; however, depending on if the mispricing falls in the favor of the trader or the writer. It is also important to keep in mind that the amount of risk that is taken on with exotic options is always going to be greater than with other options due to the limited liquidity each type of exotic option is going to have available. While some types are going to have markets that are fairly active, others are only going to have limited interest. Some are even what are known as dual-party transactions which mean they have no underlying liquidity and are only traded when two amiable traders can be found.

Not keeping earnings and dividend dates in mind: It is important to keep an eye on any underlying assets that you are currently working with as those who are currently holding calls have the potential to be assigned early dividends, with greater dividends having an increased chance of this occurrence. As owning an option doesn't mean owning the underlying asset, if this happens to you then you won't be able to collect on your hard-earned money. Early assignment is largely a random occurrence which means that if you don't keep your ear to the ground it can be easy to get caught unaware and be unable to exercise the option before you miss the boat.

Along similar lines, you are going to also always want to be aware of when the earning season is going to take place for any of your underlying assets as it is likely going to increase the price of all of the contracts related to the underlying asset in question. Additionally, you will need to be caught up on current events as even the threat of influential news can be enough to cause a significant spike in volatility and premiums as well. In order to minimize the additional costs associated with trading during these periods, you are going to want to utilize a spread. Doing so will minimize the effect that inflation has on your bottom line.

Chasing bottoms and tops: There are certainly some strategies out there that are effective when used near the turning points of existing trends. These are in the minority, however, which means that picking bottoms and tops is, more often than not, a risky proposition. Unfortunately, it is an all too common mistake for traders to invest money into securities that are either too low or too high, gleefully ignoring the 2 percent rule as they do so. This impulse should be avoided like the plague and replaced with a focus on major inbound price moves instead. Sticking to one side of markets that are range-bound will lead to better long-term results at least 90 percent of the time.

Sticking with relative trends: If a trend is already well-defined in the market then it is entirely possible that it is going to continue long enough for you to make some money off of it but it is far from a guarantee. The market will naturally fluctuate up to 20 percent of its current average with very little warning, before settling back to the current standard. This means that if you recklessly jump onto a specific trend without doing the required homework you will frequently find yourself making a momentum play that is never going to go anywhere.

Before you make a move regarding a specific trend, there are three distinct timeframes you are going to want to consider first. If you are prone to trading in the short-term then you are going to want to keep an eye on the weekly hourly and daily charts. If you prefer holding onto trades for a longer period of time then daily, weekly and monthly charts are typically going to be more useful.

CPSIA information can be obtained
at www.ICGtesting.com
Printed in the USA
BVHW091058090621
609092BV00003B/1001

9 781914 142918